MONSTERS OF MYSTERY

BY SUE HAMILTON

Published by ABDO Publishing Company, 8000 West 78th Street, Suite 310, Edina, Minnesota 55439.
Copyright ©2008 by Abdo Consulting Group, Inc. International copyrights reserved in all countries.
No part of this book may be reproduced in any form without written permission from the publisher.
ABDO & Daughters™ is a trademark and logo of ABDO Publishing Company.

Printed in the United States.

Editor: John Hamilton
Graphic Design: Sue Hamilton
Cover Design: Neil Klinepier
Cover Illustration: *Bigfoot,* ©2007 RobRoy Menzies
Interior Photos and Illustrations: p 4 Coelacanth, Photo Researchers, Inc.; p 5 Actor as yeti,
©2007 John Hamilton; p 6 Yeti skull & hand, Getty; p 7 Hillary, Corbis; p 8 *Yeti,* ©2007 RobRoy
Menzies; p 9 Snow footprint, Mary Evans; p 10 *Bigfoot,* ©2007 RobRoy Menzies; p 11 1967 Bigfoot
picture still, Corbis; p 12 *Surprised,* ©2000 RobRoy Menzies; p 13 Dale Wallace, ©2002 Dave Rubert;
p 14 *Bigfoot,* ©2007 B.M. Nunnelly; *The Legend of Boggy Creek,* courtesy Showcase Productions,
Inc.; p 15 *Road Crosser,* ©2005 RobRoy Menzies; pp 16-17 *The Fisherman,* ©2002 RobRoy Menzies;
p 18 Orangutan, Getty; p 19 Florida mystery creature, courtesy of the Sarasota County Sheriff's
Department; p 20 *Wood Pile Sasquatch,* ©2005 RobRoy Menzies; p 21 Queensland, Australia, Corbis;
p 22 Mylodon stamp, courtesy Government of Cambodia; p 23 Mylodon statue, courtesy Cave of the
Milodon Natural Monument, Chile, South America; pp 24-25 Sauropod, iStockphoto; p 26 Map of
Africa, Cartesia/Hamilton; p 26-27 Elephant swimming, Getty; p 28 Aye-aye, Photo Researchers, Inc.;
p 29 *El Chupacabras,* ©2005 RobRoy Menzies

Library of Congress Cataloging-in-Publication Data

Hamilton, Sue L., 1959-
   Monsters of mystery / Sue Hamilton.
      p. cm. -- (Unsolved mysteries)
   ISBN 978-1-59928-835-2
   1. Monsters--Juvenile literature. I. Title.

QL89.H36 2008
001.944--dc22

                              2007014558

CONTENTS

MONSTERS OF MYSTERY

What monsters make their homes high in the snows of Earth's tallest mountains? What strange and unusual creatures lurk in the dark reaches of the world's forests and jungles? Even in the 21st century, our planet holds many mysteries. The more we explore, the more we find how little we know. Folklore about legendary monsters is often exaggerated, but many people claim to have witnessed unexplainable, fantastic creatures. These strange encounters have inspired many people to search for proof that the world's elusive monsters of mystery actually exist.

Cryptozoologists are researchers who seek out mythical and unknown creatures. The name comes from the Greek word *kryptos*, which means "hidden" or "secret," and "zoologist," which means "one who studies animals." Cryptozoologists investigate the stories and rumors of cryptids, creatures for which there is not enough scientific evidence to prove they exist. The great man-beasts known as Bigfoot and the yeti are examples of the creatures these people try to find.

Another type of researcher is called a cryptobiologist. Cryptobiologists look for hidden animals, seeking out examples of species once thought extinct. Could Africa have a living dinosaur in its jungles? Some say the Mokele-mbembe is just such a creature.

There have been some successes for those scientists looking for unknown or long-dead species. Tales of the kraken, a giant squid, have been told by seafarers for centuries. In 1897, the body of one of these deep-sea creatures washed up on Anastasia Island off the coast of Florida.

Below: A coelacanth, once thought extinct, was found alive in 1938 in the waters around the Comoro Islands near Madagascar.

Above: An actor portrays a yeti. Many faked photos have made people question whether the yeti, Bigfoot, and other man-beast creatures are real, although several eyewitnesses say these cryptids do exist.

Over a century later, on December 22, 2006, a Japanese research team filmed a live giant squid. Scientists now have proof that giant squids actually live and swim in Earth's oceans.

In 1938, cryptobiologists were amazed to discover the coelacanth, a fish believed to have died out 65 million years ago. The "extinct" fish was alive and swimming in the waters of the Indian Ocean.

It seems difficult to believe that in modern times there could be creatures unknown to us. However, the world is a big place. There are parts of jungles, forests, mountains, and lakes that are yet unexplored. Could monsters be out there? There are eyewitnesses who say, "Yes!" Now the challenge is to prove it.

THE YETI OR ABOMINABLE SNOWMAN

Below: A preserved skull and hand said to be that of a yeti, or Abominable Snowman, on display at Pangboche Monastery, near Mount Everest.

Yeti, Abominable Snowman, or Metoh-Kangmi—the names all refer to a monstrous, white, gorilla-like creature that reportedly lives in the Himalayan Mountains. Yeti comes from the Tibetan word yeh-the, or "little man-like animal." In the Sherpa language, yeti translates to mean "creature of the glacier." From Western mountain climbers to native Sherpas, Nepalese, and Tibetans, many people believe they have either seen the creature or its footprints in the snow.

In looking back to ancient animals that fit the monster's description, cryptobiologists point to Gigantopithicus, a 10-foot (3-m) -tall ape that lived millions of years ago. This giant primate, believed to have died out 100,000 years ago, was an ancestor to today's orangutans. Could such a creature still be alive?

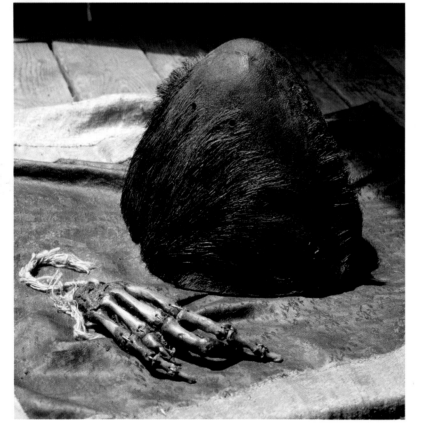

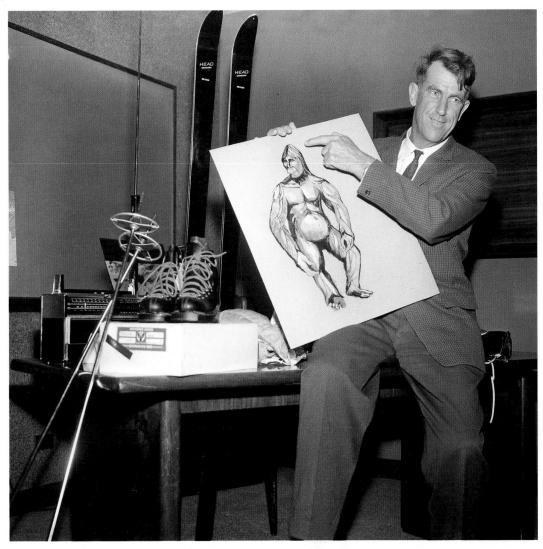

The idea of a giant ape living on a remote mountaintop is certainly intriguing. Many people have searched for the elusive yeti. In 1953, Edmund Hillary and his Sherpa guide Tenzing Norgay became the first to scale Mount Everest, the tallest mountain in the world. While on the mountain, the two men found unusually large footprints in the snow. Hillary was puzzled. What kind of creature could make such prints?

Seven years passed before the mountain-climbing legend returned to the area. He spent 10 months searching for clues to the monster's existence. In 1960, Hillary followed footprints, listened to local stories, and searched the mountains, hoping to find an actual live yeti.

Above: In January 1960, mountaineer Edmund Hillary showed a drawing of a yeti, which he hoped to capture on his trip to the Himalayas later that year. The explorer found no such animal.

RobRoy Menzies '0

Although Hillary did not find a live specimen, he returned with possible yeti fur and a yeti scalp. However, later tests proved that the fur was from a rare Tibetan blue bear. The scalp, which had been stored at a Khumjung monastery, was actually the molded skin of a serow, a goat-like Himalayan antelope. The mountaineer did, however, solve the mystery behind the huge tracks that he, and other climbers, had seen over the years.

During his time on the mountain searching, Hillary's team noticed tracks in the snow. As long as the tracks were in shade, they clearly resembled those of a fox. However, when the fox's trail moved into areas where the sun shone down on them, the tracks had melted and refrozen into long, almost human-like footprints. Repeated melting and refreezing of the snow had distorted the tracks. If a small fox's tracks could grow from 2 inches (5 cm) to nearly 1 foot (30.5 cm), it's easy to see how a larger animal's prints could become enormous. Hillary was sure that the large prints he had seen in 1953 were probably made by a bear, or even another human climber.

Facing Page: A yeti observes a column of mountain climbers.
Below: A 1951 photo of a giant footprint, taken by mountaineers Eric Shipton and Michael Ward while in the Himalayas. Shipton believed that the print was too fresh to have been enlarged or distorted by melting and refreezing.

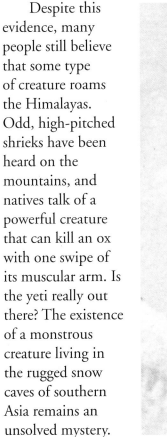

Despite this evidence, many people still believe that some type of creature roams the Himalayas. Odd, high-pitched shrieks have been heard on the mountains, and natives talk of a powerful creature that can kill an ox with one swipe of its muscular arm. Is the yeti really out there? The existence of a monstrous creature living in the rugged snow caves of southern Asia remains an unsolved mystery.

NORTH AMERICAN CRYPTIDS

They are known as Bigfoot, sasquatch, Fouke Monster, Momo, skunk ape, and more. Across the United States and Canada come tales of unusual creatures that are described as a cross between humans and giant apes. They are almost always bipedal, moving on two legs like humans. Only rarely seen, these animals reportedly live in remote forests and swamps. They are usually described as being 7 to 10 feet (2 to 3 m) tall, and weighing up to 500 pounds (227 kg). But do they really exist? Hundreds of eyewitnesses have come forward, but scientists point out they have never found any bodies, or even bones, of the elusive creatures.

Above: A still photo of Bigfoot from the 1967 16mm film shot by Roger Patterson and Bob Gimlin in Bluff Creek, California. *Facing Page:* An artistic representation of the above Bigfoot.

Bigfoot/Sasquatch

Bigfoot is the name of a creature spotted in the Pacific Northwest of North America. The term Bigfoot came from news articles referring to the creature's huge footprints. Another common name for Bigfoot is sasquatch, which is an English slurring of a word used by a Native American tribe called the Salish. In the Salish language, the word *sésquac* means "wild man."

In 1995, the Bigfoot Field Researchers Organization (BFRO) was set up to scientifically study the mysterious creature. BFRO has documented hundreds of sightings. From campers and hikers, to park rangers and scientists, many people claim they have encountered some type of huge hairy beast. As proof, there are plaster casts of footprints, recordings of howling or screeching sounds, as well as blurry photos and films. However, true encounters have often been overshadowed by pranksters.

In 1958, Ray Wallace created a Bigfoot sensation when he claimed to have discovered oversized footprints in a northern California logging camp. Over the years, Wallace became known as the "Father of Bigfoot." It wasn't until Wallace's death in November 2002 that his family discovered a pair of carved wooden feet that Wallace had used to create the oversized footprints. His joke became a media sensation that the prankster did not expect. He kept the secret until his death, when his relatives found the wooden stompers among Wallace's belongings. However, BFRO researchers have examined plaster cast prints made from those wooden feet, as well as casts of the original 1958 footprints. They are convinced that the two prints do not match. Only Wallace could say for sure, and he can no longer do that.

Perhaps the most famous piece of evidence is a 1967 16mm film shot by Bigfoot seekers Roger Patterson and Bob Gimlin. The pair had gone to Bluff Creek, California, a place known for sightings and footprints, determined to capture a Bigfoot on film. They did just that, bringing back footage of a creature walking, turning once toward the camera, and then walking on. For over 35 years, the footage seemed like positive evidence, until Bob Heironimus came forward. Bob said he was 26 years old at the time, and was hired by Patterson and Gimlin to wear a modified great-ape costume. It seemed that the footage was all a hoax. However, BFRO questioned Bob's confession. BFRO pointed out that the original Bigfoot costume has never been found, nor has anyone been able to reproduce the costume accurately, although several sources have tried.

Does the mysterious Bigfoot exist? Whether or not actual proof is found, there are a number of eyewitnesses who say some kind of creature is really out there.

Facing Page: Bigfoot in a dense forest. Many Bigfoot sightings have been reported in this type of location. *Below:* Dale Lee Wallace holds a stomper that his uncle, Ray Wallace, used to create the giant footprints found in a northern California logging camp in 1958.

Fouke Monster

The small town of Fouke, Arkansas, is reportedly home to a legendary 7-foot (6-m) -tall, hairy terror with an appetite for cows, sheep, and chickens. In the 1970s, the town received national attention after newspaper reporter Jim Powell wrote about members of a local family who had been terrorized by what he called the "Fouke Monster."

As the story goes, resident Bobby Ford had just returned home from a hunting trip in May 1971. He and his friends thought they saw something at the back of his house. Using a flashlight, the men spotted some type of creature. Shots were fired. The men thought the animal fell, but as they started towards it, a woman's screams stopped them short.

Knowing the screams came from his wife, Ford raced around to the front yard. He wasn't expecting to be met by a monstrous creature with red eyes. The animal attacked, wrapping its hairy arm around Ford's neck and shoulders. Terrified, the man broke free, running full speed right through his house's closed front door. Inside was his wife, Elizabeth, who stood terrified, having seen the creature's clawed hand reach through an open window. The Fords immediately called the local sheriff's department.

Above: The Fouke Monster terrorized the town of Fouke, Arkansas in the 1970s.

Above: 1973's *The Legend of Boggy Creek* was based on Arkansas' Fouke Monster.

A thorough search was conducted, particularly in the area where the men had thought they'd shot the creature. No body, not even any blood, was found. But they did see some odd tracks on the ground, a few broken tree branches, and claw scratches on the porch. The Fords were too frightened to stay in their home. A few days later, they moved away.

The story became national news. Researchers, monster hunters, and journalists all headed into Fouke, interviewing local residents and searching the surrounding area. Rewards were offered to anyone who could find the creature. No rewards were ever collected, but a movie was filmed. *The Legend of Boggy Creek*, part documentary and part fictional thriller, was released to theaters in 1973.

Some people wonder if Bobby Ford's attacker was a bear, or perhaps a mountain lion. Others think it was all a hoax. But some believe a Bigfoot-like creature was actually encountered. Leslie Greer, who was the county sheriff from 1967 to 1974, recalled several reports of creature sightings. He stated in an interview, "I don't know what they saw, but I do believe they saw something."

Above: Bigfoot caught in the headlights of a car. Several people reported seeing a creature like this crossing a road near Fouke, Arkansas, only days after the Ford family's encounter.

Above: The Missouri Monster, or Momo, lives near the Mississippi River in the state of Missouri.

Momo

The Missouri Monster, or Momo, is a Bigfoot-like creature reportedly living along the Mississippi River in Missouri. The hairy, smelly cryptid was first spotted in the early 1970s. On July 11, 1972, it came to national attention after it approached the Harrison family's home outside of the small town of Louisiana, Missouri.

On this day, Terry and Wally Harrison, ages 8 and 5, were playing in their yard. The boys heard a noise and looked up to see a monstrous creature, spotted with blood, and carrying a dead dog. Their screams were heard by their older sister, Doris, who was inside the house. Looking out a window, she saw the Momo standing by a tree. Doris described the creature: "Six or seven feet tall, black and hairy. It stood like a man but it didn't look like one to me." The children escaped, and the police were called.

Over the course of the next few days, other people reported loud growling noises and smelled the odd, unpleasant odor that Edgar Harrison, the children's father, said was "a moldy, horse smell or a strong garbage smell."

On July 19, Police Chief Shelby Ward and 18 others conducted a thorough search of the area. Nothing was found. However, the following day a reporter accompanied Edgar farther up the hill. There they discovered a 10-inch (25-cm) footprint and what appeared to be a 5-inch (13-cm) handprint. They decided to search an empty, rundown shack that Harrison thought might be a resting place for the Momo. Inside, they were overcome by a horrible stench. Harrison was sure the monster was nearby. But even though they immediately searched the area, nothing was found.

Over time, several other people reported seeing the beast. Cryptozoologists swarmed the area, as did television and newspaper reporters. Eyewitnesses were interviewed over and over. They described a 6-foot (2-m) -tall creature, covered in long black hair. Its head seemed to sit directly on its shoulders, as though it had no neck.

Unfortunately, nothing was ever found to prove the creature's existence. Additional sightings continued over the years. Most agree that so many eyewitness reports cannot be dismissed, but what exactly they saw is still a mystery.

Skunk Ape

Florida's Everglades are home to a creature that has become known as the skunk ape. This Bigfoot-like creature has been described as a large orangutan- or gorilla-like beast with a horrible skunky odor.

Although the creature had been sighted since the 1940s, the skunk ape received a great deal of attention on December 22, 2000. On this date, the Sarasota County Sheriff's Department received a letter and photographs from an elderly woman who had taken pictures of the skunk ape from her backyard several weeks earlier. Her husband thought the creature was an orangutan. She was concerned that it might have been someone's pet that had gotten loose.

Below: An orangutan peers from behind foliage. Some wonder if the Florida sightings of a skunk ape were really an orangutan.

Left & Below: Photos sent to the Sarasota County Sheriff's Department in December 2000. An elderly woman took the pictures in her backyard, but did not say who she was. She was concerned the creature might be an escaped pet.

The creature smelled awful and was obviously hungry, as it stole apples from a basket the woman had on her back porch. Because it was so big, she was also worried that it might attack someone. She stated, "…I judge it as being about six and a half to seven feet tall…." The woman went on to describe the general area where she lived and asked that the police start looking for the animal.

The police began searching. They issued a warning to residents of the area to stay away from the creature. They believed they were looking for a large orangutan. However, when local cryptozoologist Chris Dotson saw the pictures, he believed that they were looking for something twice as big as an orangutan—a skunk ape. Dotson stated, "People need to stay away from it, allow experts to come in who have some knowledge of large primates like this and trap this animal."

Unfortunately, orangutan or skunk ape, the animal was never found. Additional reports of a big creature in Florida continued. What was it? It's still a mystery.

Above: The cryptid yowie lives in Australia and New Zealand.

THE YOWIE

Its screams send shivers up the bravest person's back, while its smell is enough to make a stink bug turn tail and run. The howling, reeking beast is a wild resident of the down-under lands of Australia and New Zealand. Described as 6- to 7-feet (1.8- to 2.1-m) tall, with thick black or brown fur, it appears to be a close cousin to the North American Bigfoot and the Himalayan yeti. British settlers arriving in Australia in the 19th century were told of the mysterious man-monster living deep in the country's forests and mountains. In 1881, an Australian newspaper reported the sighting of a baboon-like animal that stood taller than a man. Europeans called the creatures Australian apes, yahoos, and youries, but in recent times the name "yowie" has stuck.

The creature has most recently been reported in the small Australian town of Springbrook, Queensland. The stinky gorilla-like creature has been heard and smelled much more than it has been seen. Its sounds have been described as blood-curdling screams, inhuman noises, and animal-like growls. Those familiar with the area's wildlife have never heard sounds like these.

As frightening as it sounds, it's the yowie's nasty stench that people really remember. Described as something between rotting meat and garbage, the smell is overpowering. In 1997, one woman heard something by her house. When she went outside to investigate, she nearly threw up because of the ghastly smell. Sickened, she watched some sort of 7-foot (2.1-m) -tall creature race away.

Some believe that this creature is a throwback to Australia's ancient megafauna, large mammals found in this particular area. Researchers also concede that with so much heavily forested land, it would not be surprising if an undiscovered creature exists there. However, the scientific community points to the fact that no physical evidence has been uncovered to support the claim that a yowie exists. Despite footprints and eyewitnesses, the remains of a dead yowie have never been found. Also, no photographs of the beast have ever been documented.

Is some kind of wild, horrible-smelling creature running loose in the Australian outback? Bill O'Chee, a senator in Queensland, a state in northeastern Australia, vividly recalled being on a student camping trip near Springbrook in 1977. He said, "About 20 of us saw it. It was about three meters tall, covered in hair, had a flat face and walked to the inside in a crab-like style." Is the yowie still out there? The mystery remains.

Below: A photo of the dense foliage in Queensland, Australia.

MAPINGUARI

The Amazon rainforests of Brazil and Bolivia are believed to be home to a giant ground sloth known as the mapinguari. Locals talk about perilous meetings with the enormous elephant-sized creature, which is remarkable considering the great Ice Age beast was thought to have died out 12,000 years ago. Cryptobiologists wonder if a Pleistocene survivor, a Mylodon, could still be wandering the jungles of South America.

Some accounts of the mapinguari make it seem much more mythical than real. It has been said to have backward feet, giant claws, and a second mouth in the center of its stomach. These fanciful descriptions have made researchers wonder if the beast actually does exist.

In the 1880s Ramón Lista, a man who was later to become governor of Santa Cruz province in southern Patagonia, spotted a giant, shaggy, red-haired animal. He fired his rifle at the creature, but it seemed that the bullets just bounced off. The animal disappeared into the brush.

In 1885, Herman Eberhard, a local farmer, discovered an unusual animal skin in a cave. It was covered in round, bony lumps. Could this have been the creature that Lista had seen? The bony nodules on its body could have deflected the bullets. Eberhard held onto the skin until 1897, when another naturalist saw the pelt and sent it to La Plata, a natural history museum outside of Buenos Aires, Argentina. The skin looked new, and the professionals in the museum wondered if a Mylodon was really alive and wandering the wilds of Patagonia.

Below: A 1994 Cambodian stamp showing a prehistoric animal called a Mylodon.

In 1899, the skin traveled to England for safekeeping, ending up in London's Natural History Museum. Both scientists and the general public were excited to think that such a creature could exist. Journalists, researchers, and adventurers traveled to South America on a quest to find the great beast. Although they searched the area where the skin was found, following up on legends and stories, no living Mylodon was ever discovered. It would take nearly 100 years before a true answer was found by science.

In modern times, a piece of the sloth skin underwent carbon dating. This scientific process determines the age of a once-living object. Although the skin looked fresh, in fact, the pelt was found to be roughly 10,383 years old. The cool cave environment had preserved the skin, but it was actually quite old.

It seemed that the mystery was solved, but reports of a giant sloth continued. In 1994, biologist David Oren once again began searching for the living fossil. His efforts to discover the beast have not yet been rewarded. Is a mapinguari out there? Some say no, but others continue to wonder.

Above: A full-size Mylodon statue stands near the cave where Mylodon fossils were found in Chilean Patagonia, South America.

MOKELE-MBEMBE

Could Africa be host to a living sauropod dinosaur? From deep in the swamps of Congo, Cameroon, and Gabon come tales of Mokele-mbembe, a monstrous animal whose name means "one that stops the flow of rivers." Described by local people as having a long, flexible neck, an alligator-like tail, and a body somewhere between the size of a hippopotamus and an elephant, it reportedly reaches a length of 16 to 32 feet (5 to 10 m). Mokele-mbembe lives mostly underwater, surfacing only to eat plants or to move to another location.

Right: A statue of a sauropod dinosaur. Mokele-mbembe, whose name means "one that stops the flow of rivers," is thought to look like this.

To protect itself, the creature has been known to overturn boats, and reportedly has killed humans and hippos with its teeth and tail. It does not eat its kill, however. A strict herbivore, it prefers the malombo plant as its main food source.

But does Mokele-mbembe really exist? The first record of the creature came from Abbé Lievain Bonaventure Proyart, a French priest who wrote about the Congo Basin of Africa in 1776. Proyart described finding monstrous footprints about 3 feet (.9 m) across and 7 feet (2.1 m) apart from each other.

In 1909, naturalist Carl Hagenbeck was told of a "huge monster, half elephant, half dragon" living in the Congo's swamps. Hagenbeck organized a search for the creature, but the expedition was defeated by native attacks and disease.

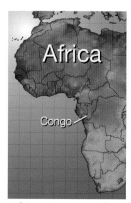

Above: A map of Africa showing the Republic of Congo. Several expeditions have searched in this area for the sauropod known as Mokele-mbembe.

In 1913, Captain Freiherr von Stein was sent by the German government to explore the Congo. Although he did not see the creature himself, he was shown a path at the Ssombo River that was reportedly created by the monster as it came up from the water to eat nearby plants.

Modern expeditions have centered their searches in the Likouala and Lake Tele regions of the Congo. Nearly unchanged since the Cretaceous Period, this 50,000-square-mile (129,000-sq-km) area is a perfect hiding place. It is filled with thick forests and wetlands. Few people and even fewer roads are found there. Scientists agree that an undiscovered large animal could possibly exist there.

In 1980 and 1981, biologist Dr. Roy P. Mackal and researcher Richard Greenwell journeyed to the Congolese jungles in search of Mokele-mbembe. While traveling by canoe, their group rounded a curve in the river, heard a splash, and saw the waves of what had to have been a large creature disappearing under the water. Their native guides were frightened and convinced that they had just missed Mokele-mbembe. Unfortunately, none of the group actually saw what caused the disturbance in the water.

Dr. Marcellin Agnagna, a zoologist and director of Wildlife and Protected Areas in the Republic of Congo, is one of the few eyewitnesses to Mokele-mbembe. In April 1983, Agnagna was on Lake Tele and encountered what he believed was a dinosaur-type creature. He grabbed his camera, but in his excitement, he forgot to remove the lens cap. Although he viewed the creature for 20 minutes, no clear pictures exist as proof of his encounter.

In 1992, a Japanese film crew flying over Lake Tele captured what some believe is 15 seconds of footage of Mokele-mbembe. From the small plane, the cameraman focused on the shape, although the footage is jumpy and blurry. Something large was moving across the surface of the lake, leaving a V-shaped wake behind it. Suddenly, the swimming animal dove under the water. Could this footage be proof?

Skeptics still wonder. It's possible that the creature people reported seeing could have been an elephant crossing the water with its trunk up. When swimming, an elephant's trunk can look like the long neck of a dinosaur. Its head or back also resembles the hump of a sauropod.

Or could the mysterious creature have been a large monitor lizard? In the water, the lizard's narrow head, long neck and tail, and sharply clawed feet could easily be mistaken for a dinosaur. In fact, monitor lizards are known to lash out their tails in a fight, just as the Mokele-mbembe has been described doing. However, quite the opposite of the dinosaur creature, monitor lizards are meat eaters. These carnivores gulp down fish, snakes, and birds whole. They wouldn't leave meat untouched in favor of plants.

Is the Mokele-mbembe an unknown dinosaur from millions of years ago, or a case of mistaken identity? The search goes on.

Below: An elephant swimming. From a distance, the trunk looks like the long neck of a sauropod, while the top of its head looks like the dinosaur's body.

CHUPACABRA

Chupacabra is a mysterious cryptid whose name means "goat sucker," or "goat vampire." It got its name after leaving puncture wounds in the bodies of dead goats, and draining the animals of their blood. First seen on the Caribbean island of Puerto Rico, chupacabra sightings have also been reported in Mexico, Nicaragua, and Chile, as well as parts of the southern United States.

Descriptions of the creature vary. Some say it looks like a small dinosaur, with sharp teeth, red eyes, and pointed quills running down its back. Others say it's more of a black panther-like creature, with big dark eyes and a long, forked tongue. However, many scientists are skeptical that such a creature exists. They believe the mysterious animal deaths blamed on chupacabra may have been caused by stray dogs, or even humans playing grisly pranks. Still, eyewitnesses claim that the creature exists.

In 1996, in the city of Canüvanas, Puerto Rico, Michael Negron watched a hopping animal leaping around his home. He reported, "It was about three or four feet tall, with skin like that of a dinosaur. It has eyes the size of hens' eggs, long fangs, and multicolored spikes down its head and back." The next morning, the creature was discovered standing over the dead body of the family's goat. The chupacabra was chased off, but it stayed in the area, attacking horses, cows, chickens, and rabbits, as well as pet dogs. Townspeople tried to capture the chupacabra, which they described as "alien-looking and kangaroo-like," with an odd sulfur-like smell to it. The beast escaped, bounding quickly away. People in this town, including the mayor, were positive that some type of unknown creature was out there.

Some people wonder if the chupacabras could have been some type of genetic experiment that escaped.

Below: An aye-aye, an endangered species native to eastern Madagascar. Some people wonder if this is the animal that has been described as a chupacabra.

Was it the result of a mixed species? Is it an entirely new breed of animal? Most researchers think that's highly unlikely.

Other theories suggest that the chupacabra could be an alien, or a vampire bat. Some people think the creature's descriptions sound like an aye-aye, an animal native to the island of Madagascar. The aye-aye is a mammal that looks like a cross between a raccoon, a bat, and a woodpecker. It has sharp, pointed teeth, and long, thin, middle fingers that allow it to pull grubs out of holes in wood. It lives high in trees, moves by leaping, and is active at night. It does not, however, live on blood. Instead, it eats nuts, fruits, grubs, and eggs. Could an aye-aye have been brought into these areas? It is possible, but the small creature only weighs about 5.5 pounds (2.5 kg) and is a mere 1 foot (30 cm) tall, not including its tail. It certainly wouldn't be attacking goats and cattle.

Could there be an unknown creature out there? Or could it be an alien? Could it be an animal from another country? Without scientific study on a living or dead specimen, the mystery remains.

Above: An artistic rendering of two chupacabras based on descriptions that say the cryptid animals have red eyes, fangs, quills on their backs, and move by hopping.

GLOSSARY

ABOMINABLE
Disgusting and very unpleasant. The phrase "Abominable Snowman" may have come from a poor rendering of a Tibetan phrase for "snowfield man."

COELACANTH
Once thought to be extinct, this large, bony fish was found alive in the waters of the Comoro Islands near Madagascar in 1938.

CRETACEOUS PERIOD
A time period from about 146 million to 65 million years ago. The weather was warm, the first flowering plants grew, and dinosaurs lived throughout the world. The Cretaceous Period ended with the abrupt extinction of the dinosaurs. The term Cretaceous comes from the Latin word *creta* which means "chalk." In 1822, Belgian geologist Jean d'Omalius d'Halloy named the era for the large amount of calcium carbonate, or chalk, that was deposited during that time by marine animals' shells. The White Cliffs of Dover are an example of such deposits.

EXTINCT
An animal or species of animals that have no living members. Dinosaurs are extinct. Occasionally, creatures that were thought to be extinct have been found alive, such as the coelacanth.

HIMALAYAS
A mountain range extending about 1,500 miles (2,414 k) along the border between India and the Tibet region of China, and through Pakistan, Nepal, and Bhutan. The Himalayas contain many of the highest mountain peaks on Earth, including Mount Everest.

MEGAFAUNA
A group of large mammals—animals that weigh more than 100 pounds (45 k)—that live or lived in a specific area, habitat, or time period. Examples of extinct megafauna include woolly mammoths, saber-toothed cats, giant ground sloths, and mastodons.

MONASTERY
A place where people of a specific religion live.

MYLODON
A giant ground sloth that lived in the Patagonia area of South America during the Pleistocene epoch, until about 10,000 years ago. The huge prehistoric mammal weighed about 440 pounds (200 k) and stood up to 10 feet (3 m) tall.

PATAGONIA
The southernmost region of South America, located in southern Argentina and Chile. The area is known for its cold temperatures and unusual wildlife.

PLEISTOCENE
A historical period of time from about 1,640,000 to 10,000 years ago. Major changes in temperature caused ice ages, which were followed by years of warmer, milder temperatures. Several forms of early humans appeared during this time.

SALISH
American Indian people who lived in the areas of the northwestern United States and British Columbia, Canada. "Salish" is also the name of the language spoken by these people.

SAUROPODS
Small-headed, long-necked, huge-bodied dinosaurs that were the largest animals ever to have lived on land. The smallest sauropods were about 20 feet (6 m) long, while the largest, Supersaurus, was as long as 130 feet (40 m). The only modern creature that comes close in size is the Blue Whale, which grows up to 110 feet (33 m) in length. Well-known examples of sauropods include the Apatosaurus, Brachiosaurus, and Diplodocus.

SHERPA
An ethnic group, originally from Tibet, that lives in the mountains of Nepal. Sherpas were valuable guides to early explorers of the Himalayas. "Sherpa" is also the name of the language spoken by these people.

TIBET
A region in central Asia within China and bordering Nepal and India. The region of Tibet has an average elevation of 16,000 feet (4,877 m), and is called the "Rooftop of the World."

INDEX